Epoxy Resin Art for Beginners

The Ultimate Step-By-Step Guide to Learn Resin Techniques and Discover Tons of Projects to Unleash Your Creativity Stress-Free

By

Anne Greson

© **Copyright 2023 by Anne Greson - All rights reserved.**

This document is geared towards providing exact and reliable information in regards to the topic and issue covered. The publication is sold with the idea that the publisher is not required to render accounting, officially permitted, or otherwise, qualified services. If advice is necessary, legal or professional, a practiced individual in the profession should be ordered.

- From a Declaration of Principles, which was accepted and approved equally by a Committee of the American Bar Association and a Committee of Publishers and Associations.

In no way is it legal to reproduce, duplicate, or transmit any part of this document in either electronic means or in printed format. Recording of this publication is strictly prohibited, and any storage of this document is not allowed unless with written permission from the publisher. All rights reserved.

The information provided herein is stated to be truthful and consistent, in that any liability, in terms of inattention or otherwise, by any usage or abuse of any policies, processes, or directions contained within is the solitary and utter responsibility of the recipient reader. Under no circumstances will any legal responsibility or blame be held against the publisher for any reparation, damages, or monetary loss due to the information herein, either directly or indirectly.

Respective authors own all copyrights not held by the publisher.

The information herein is offered for informational purposes solely and is universal as so. The presentation of the information is without contract or any type of guarantee assurance.

The trademarks that are used are without any consent, and the publication of the trademark is without permission or backing by the trademark owner. All trademarks and brands within this book are for clarifying purposes only and are owned by the owners themselves, not affiliated with this document.

Table of Contents

Introduction 6

Chapter 1: Basics of Resin Art 9

    1.1 How do you use resin? 10

    1.2 Advice for Novice Resin Crafters 10

    1.3 Making Resin Blends for Crafts 11

    1.4 Examine the resin specifications for the craft you intend to create. 12

    1.5 Types of Resin 12

    1.6 What Are the Applications of Resin Art? 16

Chapter 2: Basic Resin Crafting Techniques for Art Resin 19

    2.1 Resin Art Tool and Supply Essentials 23

Chapter 3: Epoxy Resin Projects for Beginners 33

    3.1 Craft Resin Coasters 33

    3.2 Petri Dish Coasters 36

    3.3 Gold Leaf Canvas (Poured resin) 38

    3.4 Epoxy Resin Lap Desk 40

    3.5 Bar Cart Makeover by using resin. 43

    3.6 Alcohol Ink Resin Hearts 46

    3.7 Alcohol Ink Resin Keychains 47

    3.8 Black Glitter Geode Coasters 50

    3.9 Seashell Coasters 51

    3.10 Marbled Resin Wood Coffee Table 54

    3.11 Ocean Resin Art 58

    3.12 Marbled Gold Leaf Resin Calligraphy Oblique Holders 61

    3.13 Casting Clear Resin Paperweights 64

    3.14 Maui's Fishhook Necklace 66

    3.15 Resin Gold Glitter Brunch Tray 68

3.16 Leaf Clover Shamrock Keychain of Resin 69

3.17 Sparrow Wall Art Custom Silicone Mold 71

3.18 Bottle Cap Keychains Magnets Pinbacks 74

3.19 Gold Leaf & Emerald Cabinet Knobs 75

3.20 Resin Agate Slices 77

3.21 Tree Branch Jewellery Organizer 79

3.22 Lace Pendants 81

3.23 Mermaid Tail Resin Keychains 82

3.24 Resin Succulent Garden 84

3.25 Faceted Gem Magnets 86

3.26 Beaded resin Letter 88

3.27 Colorful layered Pencil Holder 91

3.28 Resin Bookmarks 95

3.29 Wood Bookend 96

3.30 Confetti Resin Tray 99

Conclusion 101

BONUS TIME 101

Introduction

Epoxy resins are referred to as "the family of monomeric/ oligomeric materials which could be also reacted to constitute thermoset polymers that exhibit a high extent of chemical as well as solvent resistance, exceptional adhesion to a wide range of substrates, flexibility, resistance, and useful electrical properties" in the scientific world. When choosing an epoxy resin, the modifiers, resin, as well as cross-linking agent can be specifically chosen to produce unique properties for a certain application. This enables the use of epoxy resins in a wide range of applications.

High performance is a reputation for epoxy resins. They serve as the building blocks for composite materials like fibreglass, carbon fibre, reinforced plastics, adhesives, coatings, and other materials that maintain their structural stability under demanding circumstances. Epoxy resins provide several useful qualities when properly set, including:

- A defence against chemicals, especially in alkaline conditions
- Resistance to heat
- A variety of substrates' adhesion
- Strong in compression, tensile, and bend
- Little shrinkage during curing

- Corrosion protection
- A broad range of temperatures for curing

Resin art has a complex and rich significance. After all, it takes many shapes and calls for various sorts of resin.

So, before you can answer "What really is resin art?" one needs to know what resin is.

Resin is a very viscous, high-gloss substance that may be produced naturally and artificially.

There are several different viewpoints on this material because it resembles plastic in certain ways.

Most people view it as a sort of plastic, whereas others see it the opposite way, believing that plastic is merely the end product of processed resin.

In contrast, some think resin and plastic are the same.

Resin is a sticky liquid formed when trees bleed their oils in reaction to injury. When these oils are exposed to air, they oxidize, becoming resin, a thick, sticky substance.

Natural resin has been utilized since ancient Greece when it was widely used as an earlier form of chewing gum to keep breath fresh.

Resin art has, surprisingly, been around for a very long time. Often known as nature's resin, amber is generated by fossilizes and trees to form a solid, transparent slab. Decorative jewellery and decorations made of amber have been used for a long time.

Modern resin is produced artificially and utilized for comparable reasons. During the 1930s era, epoxy resin was originally identified. As soon as it became apparent that it could be used to adhere goods together and preserve various artefacts, it was patented as a separate product. Epoxy resin soon found its path into the art world, where it's been utilized ever since.

Chapter 1: Basics of Resin Art

Resin art is formed by combining a fluid chemical named epoxy resin with various colour pigments plus additives to create a unique combination of textures and patterns. The resin mixture progressively becomes a solid plastic when combined with a hardener due to a chemical interaction between its constituent parts.

Epoxy resin, a synthetic substance created to simulate the desirable qualities of natural resin, is used in resin art. The two components of epoxy resin are synthetic polymer resin as well as a hardener.

Following their combination, these elements undergo a chemical process that causes the mixture to solidify and create a solid medium.

The amount of epoxy resin you will require may be calculated with the help of the project's dimensions. The ratio of resin to hardener in resin art is typically 1:1. Prioritize precisely measuring and carefully combining the ingredients to guarantee that the final product is fully cured. The finished product is a strong, clear plastic that can be moulded into any form or pattern.

Many resin crafts have been developed for those of us who aren't as drawn to the classic paint on canvas as the extraordinary manner in which artists choreograph resin to produce compelling artworks.

You may produce mesmerizing works of art in their clarity, brightness, brilliance, and depth with resin. There are countless options for mixing colour pigments and other additives with epoxy resin to make resin paintings or casts.

Several effects may be created by selecting the painting surface, the casting method, the colours, and the additives. Even seasoned resin painters are constantly learning new things.

The United States, Canada, and Australia are leading the way in the usage of resin in art. The methods are still not well understood in Europe. Working with resin is great if you enjoy trying new things. In addition, the resin can be utilized to finish drawings, photographs, and paintings—created with oil, alcohol, ink acrylic, watercolour, ink, or other mixed media—a shine while also shielding them from UV rays and mechanical forces. You may also use epoxy to paint wood, create your epoxy river table, and make geode art.

1.1 How do you use resin?

You'll be surprised by this since it sounds too simple to be true, though it's real. Simply combine the two components, add colouring, pour, and then allow it to cure. You usually only have several minutes before your mixture starts to set, so the secret is to determine what you wish to create before you start.

1.2 Advice for Novice Resin Crafters

Start with a low-cost epoxy resin.

Why? Epoxy is typically the "easiest" to deal with and the most accommodating whenever it comes to aspects that beginners might not be familiar with, such as humidity or temperature. If you are working with epoxy within a well-ventilated space, it often also doesn't necessitate wearing a respirator mask, which is convenient.

Additionally, epoxy resin is easily accessible. Simple epoxy resins are available at most craft stores as well as online at retailers like Michael's and Amazon.com. Although they might have fewer colour options, the most affordable basic kits would be approximately USD 20. However, spending over $20 might be beyond your price range when you're just starting, so that works.

1.3 Making Resin Blends for Crafts

When you're gazing at two liquid bottles, mixing resin could seem a little frightening, but after you've done it once, you'll realize that the process is as simple as mixing, pop bubbles, pouring, and letting it set.

The "scariest" element of the project may be mixing the resin, but as far as you are able to measure precisely, stir, and pop several bubbles, you can complete this craft, whether you're constructing a massive layered piece, a little casting, or perhaps just seal-coating.

1.4 Examine the resin specifications for the craft you intend to create.

You must be aware of your resources before beginning, just like with another project. Have you ever considered that resin may change shape when heated?

For resin painters, for instance, hot cups might lead to a sticky situation. You must be aware of this before beginning since a hot cup might destroy your design if you do not use a heat-resistant resin. Additionally, because heat-resistant resin takes a little longer to cure, utilizing it might

occasionally modify your strategy. While for some people, this stage will just take a few hours or days.

1.5 Types of Resin

Resin has a wide range of applications; it may be shaped and moulded into any design or shape, used as an epoxy, or disguised or combined with other substances to adhere to or function together.

Several varieties of resin are present, each with a unique composition and set of characteristics. The hardener (catalyst) plus the base resin are the two elements that make up the majority of resins. These ingredients react chemically when combined, allowing the resin to harden as a result. UV resin is unique in that it only contains one component since it has to be exposed to UV light to start a chemical reaction that will cause your resin to set.

UV Resin

UV resin differs from other resins since it contains just one element. UV resin sets relatively rapidly because the chemical process that causes the resin to harden only has to be activated by ultraviolet light exposure.

To use UV resin, you just pour it onto the object you want to cover. If you'd like, you may tint or colour the resin before pouring it. You must expose your UV resin to UV light in order for it to cure. The thickness of a resin you have poured and the size of an item will determine how long you have to expose it to UV light.

Polyurethane Resin

Polyurethane resin is an incredibly solid material that may produce several objects, including casting moulds. When heat is applied to set polyurethane resin, it hardens and becomes exceedingly durable. Many appliances include polyurethane materials, which are frequently utilized in the automobile sector. There are many distinct forms of polyurethane resin which are employed in numerous different industries.

Epoxy Resin

With so many applications, this resin is versatile and frequently chosen for project use.

The project you are working on will dictate how you apply epoxy resin. Simply said, the fundamental application involves adding resin layers, letting each cure completely before adding the next. Once the first layer of resin has been placed, you can sand it down, but after that, no further sanding should be made between any of your subsequent applications.

Casting Resin

A specific kind of low-viscosity epoxy resin is called casting resin. Casting resin seems to have a thin consistency, which makes it a highly useful sort of epoxy resin; nevertheless, the casting resin requires longer to dry due to its thin consistency. If there is a hollow spot or region in wood or another material, casting resin can be used to fill it. Casting resin can also be used to immerse an item to preserve it.

Polyester Resin

Polyester resin may be used to create models similar to epoxy resin, although it is most frequently utilized to create ponds and swimming pools and to construct boats. The resin is strong and water-resistant, and it features a fibre structure.

Before employing polyester resin, you must mix the two components; specifically, you must add the hardener. The time required for the resin to cure depends on how much hardener is supplied. Once the two ingredients have been mixed, thoroughly mix them together, making sure that neither ingredient sinks to the bottom of your container. Once the components have been assembled, you may use the resin for laminating or creating a mould. If you have decided to create a mould, be careful to apply the coatings in a single direction. This will prevent any air bubbles from forming while the resin is applied to the glass fibre.

Which Materials Are Resin Compatible?

A wide range of materials may be used with resin. Resin often won't adhere to greasy surfaces. Molds for 3-dimensional resin art plus protected work surfaces are frequently made of substances that are incompatible with resin.

Compatible with Resin	Non-compatible with resin

Wood	Silicone
Stone	Rubber
Metal	Vinyl
Flowers	Parchment
Oil paints	Greasy surfaces
Dried acrylic	Wax paper
Photographs	Hot glue
Inkjet prints	Sheathing
	Polyethylene, polypropylene plastic
	Duct tape

1.6 What Are the Applications of Resin Art?

Artists have given their works fresh life by utilizing resin's special properties. Its tremendous degree of adaptability is among its most appealing qualities. Artworks can be made by pouring the resin over a suitable surface or in a silicone mould. Here are some examples of possible applications for resin art:

Wooden resin artwork: Epoxy resin solidifies to create a sturdy, long-lasting medium. This has made it more common to decorate ordinary hardwood furniture with resin to create distinctive pieces. Alternatively, the resin may be blended with wood chippings and pigments to resemble natural components like the ocean.

Picture art: Resin could be utilized as any protective coating for pictures because of its compatibility with a variety of dried inks. This keeps precious memories safe by preventing UV rays from losing their pigments. Instead of using traditional frames, choose resin magnets, coasters or bookmarks to display special occasions.

Jewellery and ornaments: Tinier silicone moulds can be used to make delicate resin jewellery or decorations. These artworks frequently include natural components like flowers, shells, or valuable stones. Personalized resin items are wonderful presents for loved ones, co-workers, or acquaintances.

Crockery: Since resin art may be used as dishware, it could brighten up your upcoming dinner party. Although resin cannot be put in the dishwasher, it may be cleaned with warm, soapy water. It is possible to construct gorgeous items that will wow your visitors using moulds for vases, cups, and plates.

Is Resin a Safe Material to Work With?

In general, because epoxy resins are non-toxic, consuming them does minimal harm. The hardening agents, however, are deemed harmful.

Due to their high alkaline content, some hardeners, including aliphatic polyamines, can burn the skin and create lesions. This can occasionally result in epoxy eczema. Polyamides and amino adducts are more secure substitutes.

Therefore, it is advised that you wear long sleeves and safety gloves (safety gloves seem to be a necessity) while dealing with epoxy resins to prevent skin irritation.

If the mixture accidentally gets on your skin, wash the area using warm, soapy water to remove it before it solidifies.

Epoxy resins are non-volatile; therefore, inhaling them poses no significant risk. Epoxy resin doesn't smell, which may give you the impression that it is safe to breathe in, even if it is not.

The hardeners frequently have a pungent smell that might irritate the respiratory system. Therefore, when making resin art, you could use a breathing mask.

Aside from that, amine hardeners are especially corrosive. Protect your workspace from potential harm by using a plastic drop cloth or working on a surface that you don't mind getting dirty or stained.

Chapter 2: Basic Resin Crafting Techniques for Art Resin

Straight Coating

You're pouring or painting your resin over something else to provide a thin layer of protection for the item beneath. This technique may be used for a variety of things, such as:

- Furniture
- Metal
- Dishes and glassware

You do not have to cover the entire object; only pick the required areas. Remember that unless you use food-safe materials, you shouldn't apply resin directly on food surfaces, including plates or cups. Prioritize basic safety.

Free pouring

One of my favourite approaches is this one. Have you ever considered creating art resin without a mould? No! You don't.

The resin may be poured over various items; however, it cannot be used to create 3-D objects without a mould. Consider objects such as cutting boards, boards, canvas (resin painting) and spoons. There are countless options!

The resin is poured more like a painting, which is the nicest part. As a result, it's a more creatively free-form process, making it more enjoyable than repeatedly moulding the same thing.

Layering Resin

Building up your artwork like a tiered cake by layering resin would be a crazy and entertaining approach to creating a resin design.

The fundamental layering technique involves covering an object/item you wish to treat with a resin layer. Once it has dried, add another layer over the top and continue until the required thickness is achieved. So fun!

Adding inclusions (leaves, dried flowers) to the resin between layers gives the art piece a three-dimensional effect, and you may paint directly on top of the resin to create depth.

Molding Resin

The fundamental method for working with art resin in crafts is moulding. Molds allow you to create a wide variety of 3D objects for a variety of uses. Additionally, you may create your own moulds! But that's a topic for another conversation.

Resin moulding is quite simple. Although moulding may seem difficult, all that is required is the pouring of resin into the mould. Choosing the appropriate resin mixture volume to fit your mould is the most difficult step. However, simply fill your mould using water, then count how much water there is in that amount. So simple!

Just be sure to properly dry your mould before pouring your resin inside.

Inclusions

A fundamental resin-making method is inclusions. In essence, you want to incorporate a layer into your design that will offer colour plus texture when injected into the mould. Consider adding glitter, confetti, and little plant parts to your creation if you want to give it some character.

Colouring Resin

The fundamental method for colouring resin involves mixing a colourant into the liquid before pouring.

For instance, you could wish to include a dye/ metallic shimmer that will mix with your resin and modify the colour of the resin when it has dried. This sort of simple procedure requires some experimentation but produces amazing outcomes!

Popping Bubbles

Popping bubbles is one of the silliest and most enjoyable aspects of creating resin crafts. You may have witnessed other craftsmen utilize a vacuum chamber or a butane torch, but we're referring to advanced-level techniques here; rather, we are talking about fundamental ones.

So, without all of this, how can we pop bubbles? Easy

We'll warm the resin's surface there in mould or on the surface where it was poured by utilizing a heat gun or blow dryer.

Using your stir stick to gently pop bubbles on the surface is another method of popping them.

How to Cure Resin Correctly

Art resin crafting requires curing, which is an essential phase that many overlook because they become preoccupied with other aspects of their creation. But it's crucial to cure your work, like any other activity you could complete at home.

Even though it sometimes seems like it takes an eternity to cure resin, the wait is worthwhile. It dries the work thoroughly (as opposed to merely on the surface), giving you a strong result. And keep in mind that if you do not cure your pieces properly, they can only survive for 1 or 2 years.

So how does resin become cured? Thus, all that is required is for you to leave it unattended. You're fine to go as long as the humidity, temperature, and other environmental factors remain constant.

2.1 Resin Art Tool and Supply Essentials

Applying a layer of epoxy resin on an artwork piece would be an easy way to start with epoxy resin and get a feel for that. A few simple (but important) tools are required when dealing with epoxy resin. Here are the materials you will require to apply epoxy resin as the surface coating in more detail:

Gloves

Gloves that are disposable will protect your hands. Art Resin is sticky in liquid form; thus, wearing gloves prevents a mess from forming on your hands as well as potential skin rashes. When dealing with resin, ensure you have multiple pairs of gloves.

Old clothes/Apron

While working, use an apron, old clothes or a smock to protect the clothing from the resin drips. If you accidentally spill any resin on your clothes, it is difficult to get it off. To prevent the resin from getting into your hair and the hair from getting into the resin, ponytail your long hair.

Plastic Drop Sheet

Use the plastic drop sheet for protecting your worktable and floor from the drips/ resin spills. Resin drips may be cleaned using paper towels as well as isopropyl alcohol, or if left to dry, they can be scraped off the following day. A smooth, transparent vinyl shower curtain offers a cheap, durable liner that can be utilized again. Kitchen parchment paper is ideal for smaller projects.

Masking tape

If you wish to resin the edges of your piece, just tape off from the bottom with good-quality painter's tape. This will prevent drips from ruining your artwork. Due to gravity, drops will begin to build up around the bottom as the resin drips down the sides. The tape will catch these drips, and after the resin is touchable dry, you may remove the tape and the drips together.

Stands

The excess resin might collect on the work surface if you support your artwork on plastic stands.

Level

Verify the horizontality of your work with a standard level or mobile phone level (Art Resin's). Due to the self-levelling nature of epoxy resin, if your item is tilted, it will run down the sides just at the lowest point.

Water Bath Plastic Container

If the resin you're working with is warm or cold, a water bath will reheat it to room temperature and make it simpler to handle. Pick a narrow container with high edges to prevent your bottles from tipping. The sealed bottles should soak in the warm water for ten to fifteen minutes after its been filled halfway, as warm in temperature as you could utilize for some baby's bath. After properly drying your bottles, you're prepared to measure and combine them.

Stir Stick

The best stirring equipment for resin features a flat surface; an improperly blended resin won't cure correctly, so ensure to scrape the bottom and sides of the container while you stir to ensure

that all of the hardener and resins are blended. Compared to something spherical, like a spoon, a stir stick with a flat edge can scrape a container considerably more efficiently. Tongue depressors made of wood can be used, but they must be thrown away after each usage.

Mixing Containers

Use a plastic, graded measuring jug to correctly measure or mix your resin since poorly measured resins and hardeners won't cure. This makes it crucial to pick a cup containing proper delineated lines to avoid guesstimating. As long as all components are precisely the same amount, it doesn't matter whether you measure your resin or the hardener first. Pick a plastic mixing cup, and after you're done, flip it over onto a surface covered in plastic to allow the resin to collect. Once the resin has dried the next day, you may peel it off and then reuse your cup.

Spreader

Epoxy resin can self-level once you pour it, but using a plastic spreader featuring a flat edge will help you spread it out evenly.

A little spatula and perhaps the plastic takeout knife does extremely well to push the resin all the way towards the edge without tipping over if you'd want it to sit nicely in a dome over the top of the artwork without pouring over the edges.

You can use a foam brush or gloved hands to apply resin towards the sides of an item.

Torch

A flame torch is the finest method for obtaining a perfect, bubble-free finish. Numerous bubbles appear when the resin gets mixed; if not removed, these bubbles would cure into your art piece. It is ineffective to blow them out with a straw or prick them with a toothpick. Hairdryers don't heat up to a hot enough temperature, which can blow your resin about and add dust. When utilizing silicone resin or moulds containing alcohol ink, a heat gun would be a handy tool to have on hand.

Toothpicks

When resining, toothpicks are a necessity. After torching your item, hold it to the light at eye level to check for stray bubbles and fish out any hair or dust particles. They come in helpful if you need to move tiny bits of resin or to precisely place inclusions like gems or gold flakes.

Dust Cover

Before beginning to resin, prepare a dust cover since you never would like to leave your newly resined artwork exposed while searching for a plastic tote or cardboard box. Be careful to wipe the

cover down to eliminate any dust that could fall into your wet component. We choose plastic totes since they are simple to clean. In order to prevent a flap from dropping into your resin and then curing the next day, you may utilize a cardboard box, but only if you separate the flaps.

Paper towels and alcohol

The two most crucial materials for the spill clean-up include isopropyl alcohol and paper towels. While wearing gloves, clean much of the wet resin using paper towels first, and afterwards, spritz your equipment with alcohol to get rid of leftover residue. Repeat this process till there is no residue, afterwards wipe dry with an extra paper towel. Resin should never be flushed down the toilet! When all resin residue has been removed from your tools, wash them in hot, soapy water, then let them dry completely before using them again.

Hand Cleaner

If you have sticky hands, use an exfoliating hand cleanser. If you accidentally get Art Resin onto your skin, immediately wash it off to avoid any skin irritation. The hardware store's exfoliating hand cleanser works great. The resin may be removed from your hands by dry rubbing them with a tiny bit of poppyseeds, salt, and a little liquid soap, followed by thorough rinsing with water.

Silicone Molds

Silicone moulds are ideal for tiny resin art projects since they are flexible and easy to remove from resin cast, unlike rigid plastic moulds that might rip or distort. You may use them again and time again since it returns to their original shape. Molds come in almost every size and form, but creating resin coasters within a mould such as this one is a simple job, to begin with. You could include inclusions such as shells, beer caps, decorative stones, crystals, gems, and much more.

Colourants

When coloured, epoxy resin has a lovely appearance; for optimal effects, always use a colourant made especially for resin, such as Resin Tint liquid colourant. Once the resin has reached a single, uniform tint, stir in the colourant.

Stir sticks and plastic cups.

Mix tinted resin with popsicle sticks and plastic drinking glasses: If you're doing a resin art creation with tinted resin, follow these steps:

The resin needed for the complete project should be combined in one large batch.

Depending on how much resin you need for each tint, portion it out into separate cups. For each colour, use a different cup.

After adding the tint and carefully mixing, the resin should be one uniform colour. You could always add additional colour if you begin with less than you believe you need.

Pulling a small amount of coloured resin onto the side of a plastic cup will allow you to gauge the colour's intensity and, if required, add a bit more colour.

Metal Trays & Wood Panels

Strong, solid substrates best sustain the resin weight: epoxy resin is heavy; wood panels are just an excellent choice for working with resin. For a contemporary aesthetic, mount prints, pictures, or even paint straight onto the panel, then cover it with resin. When pouring coloured resin for the ocean art/ flow art, cradled wood panels are an excellent choice since they have a lip to hold the resin in place. Serving trays made of metal are also excellent for this use.

Hairdryer and Heat Gun

Use one hair dryer for the flow art and a heat gun for the silicone moulds; while we nearly always advise using the flame torch, there seem to be three exceptions:

When using alcohol ink, be aware that alcohol is flammable & that using a flame torch might result in a fire. In most instances, alcohol inside the ink would dissolve many bubbles of resin on its own; however, if you want more assistance, a heat gun is acceptable.

A heat gun would be a useful substitute for a flame while dealing with silicone moulds because a flame's intensity runs the risk of destroying the material. Use a heat gun/hair dryer on low to gradually press the layers of coloured resin, generating fascinating effects for making cells and lacing for flow art. Finish by passing a flame torch over the surface to quickly remove any bubbles.

Inclusions

Include gold leaf, crystals, ornamental stones, charms, glitter, and other fun small embellishments in your work to give sparkle, intrigue, and texture. . You may dangle gold leaf flakes, add crushed glass/ crystals resembling geodes, put in glitter for depth and brightness, or make coasters out of dried flowers, shells, or bottle caps. There are literally a million various items you can introduce to the resin at the craft shop; always ensure your inclusions are completely dried.

Sandpaper

You could occasionally discover that your resin has hardened but still contains a bubble, some dust, or even hair. Don't worry; this may be quickly repaired by applying a new resin coat. To prepare the initial coat so that the new resin will have something to stick to, you must sand it down first. Use a rough sandpaper, say 80 grit, across the whole surface, whether you're using a sandpaper piece, a sanding block and an electric sander. Pay special focus to sanding out the trouble spot. It will appear to be a mess, but don't be concerned. It will seem as good as new once you remove all the sanding dust & apply your new coat.

Chapter 3: Epoxy Resin Projects for Beginners

3.1 Craft Resin Coasters

Supplies

- Glaze Coat Craft
- Clear bumpers
- Silicone coaster moulds
- Dust covers (or parchment paper)
- Items of choice to embed.
- Butane lighter (i.e., for popping bubbles!)
- Drop cloth (for spills)
- Latex gloves
- Disposable measuring cups plus larger plastic cups for mixing the resin in
- Wooden stir sticks

Instructions

- When working, pick a place that is well-ventilated and protect the surface with a mat or drop cloth. Put on your safety gloves next. If you are cautious, this procedure should not be messy, but it's crucial to have things covered in a spill.

- Grab a trash can and remove the packing from all of your supplies. Additionally, be sure to read your Glaze Coat Craft directions well at this time and keep them handy, so you can return to them again later.

- You simply need a little resin for this initial coat. Just enough is present to serve as glue for the objects you are embedding. I used about 60ml from each bottle, which was more than enough for 4 coasters.

- Glaze Coat Craft has the advantage of being a straightforward 1:1 mixing ratio. It requires some time because there are two 6-minute-long mixing stages, but it was quite simple, and the directions were extremely clear. You may set a timer over your phone to maintain track of the passing of time.

- When mixing time is finished, pour a little amount of resin into every mould. In each mould, carefully push the materials you are embedding. I utilized moulds with built-in rims, so I had to embed everything upside down to ensure it'd be right facing up when it was flipped over.

- Even though there won't be many bubbles at this point, you can still explode them with a butane lighter by moving them over the entire area while staying at a minimum of 6 inches above the surface.

- As soon as you are finished, cover the moulds with the dust cover and leave them alone for about four hours to enable the first layer to cure.

- The procedure for the fill coat is the same as previously; you just need to mix up a lot greater amount of your Glaze Coat Craft. We poured the resin and hardener into a larger disposable cup since the measuring cups were too small for mixing. For this step, I used about 180ml per bottle.

- After finishing both mixing steps, gently pour the mix into each mould.

- At this point, there are probably a couple more bubbles for you to pop. The glaze would start to set if you left them for more than 15 minutes. It appeared to work best to keep them for five min to let your bubbles rise towards the surface. It turns out that this could have been the most enjoyable step in the procedure since popping all these bubbles is quite fulfilling!

- When you are happy with how these coasters appear, cover them with the dust cover once again and keep them rest for a minimum of 24 hours. It's recommended to avoid touching it at this point to avoid leaving unsightly fingerprints on your coaster's bottom!

- The complete curing process might take up to 72 hours. The mould simply peels off since it is flexible, revealing a gorgeous, lustrous, smooth surface below.

- Simply attach bumpers towards the bottom of every coaster to finish your craft, then sit and revel in your accomplishment.

3.2 Petri Dish Coasters
Supplies

- Clear Casting Epoxy
- Alcohol Inks
- Measuring Cups
- Silicone Coaster Mold (Hexagon)
- Disposable Gloves
- Stirring Sticks

Instructions

- Pour-On Resin should be prepared. Put on disposable gloves and add resin and hardener in equal amounts. Using a stir stick, combine it for 2 minutes, scraping the bottoms and sides and bottom of the cup as you go. Using one clean stir stick, stir the resin inside the second mixing cup for an additional minute.

- I suggest combining 5 oz of hardener and resin in total to create only 3 coasters.

- Place something, such as newspaper or a silicone mat, to safeguard your work surface. Make sure not to overfill the moulds; carefully pour resin onto each. After one minute, remove all air bubbles that have risen to the top with a straw / lighter.

- Pick your preferred shades of alcohol ink, then drop by drop, cover the uncured resin with ink. Avoid using excessive amounts of ink or mixing murky colours (green/red, blue/orange, etc.). Wear gloves and cover your workplace since alcohol inks may stain your surfaces and hands.

- The key component is white alcohol ink. It pushes through the resin since it is heavier than the coloured inks, creating this amazing appearance. The middle of each drop of coloured ink should have one drop of white added. Add another ink drop over the white once more, then repeat the process. As you progress, the ink would spread out. Avoid adding too much ink, despite how tempting it may be. It may interfere with the resin's ability to cure and muddy your coasters.

- After you've finished adding ink, just let the resin dry for 12 to 24 hours inside an even, undisturbed location.

- When the resin stops being sticky, it has reached its cure. Take care when removing the coasters from mould, and then take a moment to appreciate your accomplishment.

3.3 Gold Leaf Canvas (Poured resin)
Supplies

- High gloss resin
- Heat gun/ torch
- Variety of canvas (18×10 or 34×4)
- Stirring sticks
- Disposable work surface,
- Acrylic craft paint (desired colours)
- Gold leaf and gilding adhesive
- Mixing cups
- Liquid leaf/gold paint
- Gloves

Instructions

- Start by using a paper or disposable tablecloth to cover your workspace. Placing the canvases on cups, cans, or any other riser will make them stand out more.

- Next, combine your High Gloss resin as directed on the packaging.

- Have your paints prepared to add to the resin.

- Add a little bit of craft paint and a small quantity of resin in smaller cups. Thoroughly combine the resin and paint.

- The enjoyable part now is to begin pouring coloured resin onto the canvas. Lifting and tilting the canvas will cause the resin to flow to the edges, swirling the colours of the resin.

- More resin should be poured over each canvas. The resin should be pushed to each edge using a mixing stick.

- Continue to add resin in broad ribbons, blobs, or stripes.

- Use one heat gun to warm up the resin after it has been poured into the canvas and to move it about a bit. It will blow the resin about and pop the bubbles like one blow dryer.

- The workstation now begins to resemble a catastrophe! You can put some of your resin on that table to the canvas by picking it up with mixing sticks. Typically, 20 to 30 minutes after the resin has been mixed, it should be all in place and prepared to set. Allow the resin to set and cure overnight.

- Paint the canvas' margins gold using liquid leaf or plain paint since resin has dripped down them all.

- There is no denying that the shine of the resin is magnificent, but adding an additional gold leaf would be the ideal finishing touch. Apply gilding adhesive on the canvases using paint. Use this to hide any flaws or to follow the natural resin lines.

- Once the glue has cured and become sticky, apply the gold leaf over the top of it. Flaky and wonderful gold leaf. To remove any loose particles, dust with a stiff paintbrush.

- The painting is finally prepared for hanging on the gallery wall, ideal for a peaceful space in the house.

3.4 Epoxy Resin Lap Desk
Supplies

- Lumber
- Heat gun/butane torch
- Miter Saw
- Wooden stir sticks
- Pocket Hole Jig
- Foam brush
- Pocket hole screws (1¼")

- Epoxy mixing cups (disposable)
- Wood glue
- Masking tape
- Glaze coat
- Power Drill
- Unicorn spit (various colours)
- Random orbital sander

Instructions

- If the wood surface is brand-new, you may just sand it smooth and omit this step.
- If you plan to use an old item, clean it up, then remove any unnecessary paint or stain.
- Use a foam brush for applying Unicorn Spit with Rustic Reality as a foundation stain colour.
- Next, using a rag, remove any remaining discolouration.
- A smooth, consistently stained lap desk was the product.
- Cover the remaining portion of your tabletop using masking tape if you wish to colour roughly a third of it in jewel tones.
- Use tape with ragged and uneven edges to get a "live edge" appearance.

- Choose vibrant jewel-toned colours for the "pour" and add a touch of white to level it out.
- All the colours were zigzaggedly poured on top at random to equalize their proportions.
- Then, use a foam brush for mixing.
- Take off the tape and leave it to cure overnight.
- Apply a glaze layer to the top to preserve and give it a wonderful shiny appearance.

Glaze coat

- Inside a mixing cup, combine resin and hardener in an equal ratio for six minutes.
- Transfer to a fresh cup, then stir for six minutes.
- Apply it with a foam brush to the surface.
- Be careful to press it over the edges, so it drips and coats the whole edge.
- Use a heat gun to eliminate bubbles.
- Use your foam brush to clean up any extra epoxy spilt from the edges while turning into tiny droplets.
- To keep against dust and debris, cover and preserve in an isolated area.
- It takes around 72 hours for the glaze coat to fully cure.

- The self-levelling glaze layer dries to a stunningly smooth, glossy finish.

3.5 Bar Cart Makeover by using resin.
Supplies

- Paint Colors (Deco Art)
- Paintbrushes
- Disposable Cups
- Coloured Stones
- Gold Foil
- Metallic Gold Paint
- Mod Podge
- Lite Resin

Instructions

- Purple and pink paints are used to decorate the bar cart's top shelf.
- Fill a single disposable cup with an equal amount of each colour.
- Simply put each colour on top of the one before it.
- You don't stir it; you just leave the colours to be.

- Use greens in every shade, from dark to bright, for the 2nd level.
- Apply the same technique to the pink and stack each paint colour in a cup.
- The bottom level, the third and last one, would have an all-blue coloured scheme at the end.
- White and gold were the two colours that they all shared.
- Make sure the space you will be working in is properly covered in plastic sheets before you begin the marbling process since things may quickly become messy!
- Pour over the top-level pink/ purple paint colours while tilting the bar cart to create the marbled effect.
- Before going on to the following shelf, let it dry fully.
- The top shelf should be dry first because you wouldn't want paint from your upper shelf to leak down onto the 2nd shelf when you go to the 2nd level to create the marbled effect.
- So, only advance to your next level until the previous one is entirely dried.
- The blue one was the last.
- Once the marbling is finished, use some gold foil to make tiny flakes that you can then randomly scatter throughout the shelves.

- Several colourful stones should be used last.

- Apply a little Mod Podge to adhere them to the marbling-painted shelves together in a pattern that echoed the paint's movement.

- Loved the way it seemed so far, but the colours continued to appear flat, which is when the Lite Resin comes into play.

- To get the ideal consistency of the resin, you must use exactly equal amounts of each of the two bottles that come with it.

- The hardener is in one bottle, while the resin is in the other.

- Two full cups are needed to cover a shelf, making a total of six cups needed to cover the whole bar cart.

- Then, all that had to be done was to pour it onto the shelves.

- Even though the product claims to create the appearance of Sixty coats of varnish, it is exact. You only need to level that off slightly to ensure that every inch is entirely coated.

- The things put on top mirror themselves in the resin finish, literally.

- The final phase involves painting the handles, wheels, and border of shelves with this lovely Old Gold colour.

- Finally, it was it.

3.6 Alcohol Ink Resin Hearts

Supplies

- Alcohol Inks

- Heat Gun

- Epoxy Resin Kit

- Optional: Metallic Mixatives - Alcohol Ink

- Silicone Mold (Heart Shaped)

- Optional: Glitter

Instructions

- Calculate the amount of epoxy resin you require to mix by using water. Measure the volume of water needed to fill one of the heart-shaped cavities in your silicone mould to the required height. For hearts that were about half an inch thick, I filled the cavities halfway. Depending on how many cavities you wish to fill using resin, double the water quantity by that number. For instance, if you wish to build six hearts and each heart-shaped cavity can accommodate a half ounce of water, you will have to combine Three ounces of resin.

- Prepare the resin in the necessary quantity in accordance with the instructions on the box.

- Pour the resin mix slowly into the silicone moulds till it reaches the desired thickness or height.

- Fill each heart with 5 to 10 drops of the preferred alcohol ink colour (and metallic mixative). The colours will naturally spread. Add a little bit of glitter, if desired, to each heart.

- Any bubbles that might have developed upon the resin's surface can be gently popped with a heat gun.

- Give the resin hearts twenty-four hours to solidify.

- Once the resin gets hardened, you must be able to simply "pop" out the hearts from the silicone mould.

3.7 Alcohol Ink Resin Keychains
Supplies

- Clear Casting Epoxy
- Key Rings
- Mold Conditioner
- Jewellery Pliers
- Release Spray
- Measuring Cups

- Jewellery Chain
- Stirring Sticks
- Jump Rings
- Disposable Gloves
- Jewellery Mold
- Alcohol Inks

Instructions

- Follow the instructions on the packaging to prepare the Clear Casting Epoxy. Wear disposable gloves and make sure you are working inside a well-ventilated location. Resin and hardener should be added to the mixing cup in equal amounts.

- Make careful to scrape both sides and bottom of your mixing cup after stirring the resin mix using a stir stick for approximately two minutes. Pour the resin into a cleaned mixing cup, then stir it using a cleaned stick for a further minute or two. Use Mold Release & Conditioner to spray on mould.

- Since using alcohol inks might be a little messy, prepare your work surface by placing something on it. Make use of a stir stick to slowly pour resin onto each of your moulds. Make every effort to avoid overfilling the moulds. Allow the resin to remain for a minute before using a toothpick, straw, or lighter to zap any air bubbles which have risen to the surface.

- Add a single drop of alcohol ink to the uncured resin. Avoid using excessive amounts of ink or mixing muddy colours (blue/orange, red/green, etc.). Alcohol inks would stain your hands as well as surfaces, so shield your workplace and wear gloves.

- The magic is produced with white alcohol ink. Given that white alcohol ink is heavier than resin, it pushes through to create the amazing "petri dish" look. To the middle of each drop of coloured ink, add a drop of white ink.

- Over the droplets of white ink, add one additional drop of colourful ink. Every drop of the ink will cause it to spread. Avoid adding too much ink, despite how tempting it may be. It can muddy up the pendants and affect how the resin cures. Allow your resin to cure for 12 to 24 hours in a suitable place.

- After carefully removing the pendants from the mould, smooth any rough edges with coarse grit sandpaper and appreciate your accomplishment.

- An open jump ring may be inserted into the pendant's hole with jewellery pliers. No issue if your pendant mould has no hole in it. A drill and a little drill bit can be used to add a hole. Just ensure the hole is big enough to accommodate a jump ring.

- You may use these keychains as zipper pulls or keychains for your keys. As an alternative, you may combine the pendants to make a unique necklace.

3.8 Black Glitter Geode Coasters

Supplies

- Alcohol ink (black)
- Wood slices (4" – 4)
- Glitter black, gold
- FolkArt Treasure Gold

Instructions

- Apply painter's tape to the edge of a wood cookie, extending it at a minimum of 1/2" beyond the wood's surface. By circling the slice with your finger, ensure the tape is as close to the wood slice's sides as possible.
- Mix resin as directed on the box.
- In a different cup, add 1/4 of the resin. Add one tbsp of gold glitter to the cup.
- Include 2 drops of your black alcohol ink into the cup containing the most resin.

- Apply a thin coating of black resin within the tape to the wood slice (s). Pour first around the outside and then within.

- The middle of a wood slice should be covered with some black glitter (s).

- Pour some resin in the shape of a ring around the iridescent glitter within the middle using gold glitter resin. As you work your way around the wood slice, keep adding gold glitter resin, black resin, and loose black glitter until you have the desired effect. Pour black resin there to complete.

- Remove bubbles. As directed on the packaging, let the resin cure.

- Take off the tape from the wood slice once the resin has cured. Using sandpaper, eliminate any ambiguities (where the tape might have folded, or the resin overflowed within spots, etc.).

- Paint gold around the wood slices/borders resins with a flat brush.

3.9 Seashell Coasters
Supplies

- Jar lid (3¼" - 3½" diameter) 1
- Toothpicks

- Seashell chips
- Protective gloves
- Large shell
- Protective goggles
- Small shells
- Timer
- Pearls
- Paint stirring sticks (2)
- Felt pads, self-adhesive (4 optional)
- Spray paint, silver
- Straight-sided cups 4
- Clear silicone adhesive
- Pour-on finish (envirotex lite) (resin plus hardener kit)

Instructions

- Your jar lids should be cleaned, dried, and sprayed with silver paint. Stick the felt pads on the lids' bottoms.
- We applied the covers on delicious Pirouette cookies. But we didn't pick them for that reason. They are not threaded, which we believe is attractive. Salsa jar lids are another option.

- Glue a huge shell first into the lid of each coaster. Ensure the shell doesn't protrude beyond the jar lid's edge. We made sure the lid didn't come into contact with the shell by sliding a ruler over its top edge. Pour in enough shell chips to cover the lid's bottom and the area around the shell. Surround the central shell with smaller ones. We also included a few pearls.

- You may now begin mixing the resin. Prepare your materials, put on your gloves, and put on your safety glasses.

- Make sure that the two cups contain an equal amount of resin and hardener by pouring them into opposite cups. We used two three ounces of blended resin for each of the coasters. We divided the resin into two batches for easier handling. We measured three ounces of resin plus three ounces of hardener into two cups to produce the first batch. This amount is sufficient to cover two seashell coasters.

- After carefully measuring the resin plus hardener, combine their total contents in the 3rd cup. Set a two-minute timer to begin stirring. Utilizing a paint stirrer, combine the resin, scraping off the resin from the stick and adding it back into the mixture as you go. Pour the combined resin into a 4th clean cup after two minutes.

Using a fresh paint stirring stick, mix once more for one minute.

- Fill the seashell coasters with resin. We prefer to spray it liberally all over to ensure that it reaches every nook and corner. Pour up to the lid's top lip. Ensure a flat surface for the coasters. When they are curing, they prefer to cover them to keep dust from accumulating.

- Little bubbles would start to emerge in the coasters within five-fifteen minutes after the resin had been poured. These are normal and necessary parts of the procedure. To let the bubbles out, softly exhale over the coaster's surface. (The carbon dioxide causes the bubbles within your exhaled breath.) The large bubbles can be popped with a toothpick. Pop any trapped bubbles you find close to the shells.

- Allow the coasters to dry for 48 hours on a flat surface away from dust.

3.10 Marbled Resin Wood Coffee Table
Supplies

- Agate Crystal Slices
- Wood 2ft cross 4ft
- Resin
- Hairpin Legs

- Mod Podge
- Foam Paintbrush
- Paint
- Automatic Hand Drill
- Glitter
- Masking Tape
- Wood Stain

Instructions

- Choose paint that is a combination of the colours blue, grey, green and metallic gold.
- Pour the majority of the colours into disposable cups and thin them out to ensure they will marble easily.
- The exciting part of marbling is when you pour each colour of paint one at a time onto the wood panel, raise it at an angle, and then move it about to produce the marbled pattern.
- To create beautiful marbling details, repeat the process on the opposite side, pour the paint, and move it about.
- Dry it off.
- The Agate Slices should then be adhered to with Mod Podge/ E6000 after removing the masking tape from the centre.

- The Agate Slices came in a variety of colours, including this stunning Burnt Orange, Emerald Green, and Sky Blue.
- These Slices enhanced our Marbling Paint Colors beautifully.
- Each slice should have glue applied to it before being glued to the centre of a coffee table.
- Use glitter to add more details and shine.
- Pour enough Mod Podge together into the disposable cup before adding glitter to render the glitter enough "pour-able."
- Put the Mod Podge/ glitter mixture in a zip-top bag after mixing it all together.
- Create marbling lines by cutting a very little corner off the zip lock. This tip will make it simple for you to achieve the marbled glitter appearance as a piping bag.
- It took a day for the glitter to dry completely.
- The coffee table's side panels should be attached in order to begin pouring the resin.
- The idea behind using resin was to thoroughly seal in the agate slices & glitter while also giving it a stunning glass-like finish.

- The wood panels were fastened on all 4 corners to act as a wall for resin and prevent spills.

- Purchasing a large gallon-size container would be extremely practical and effective. You must strictly follow the package's directions when using this resin if you want the ideal glossy appearance.

- Before you're able to attach your Hairpin Legs and then stain the coffee table's sides, the resin must nearly completely cure for 72 hours.

- Attach those stunning Teal legs to the coffee table since the colour goes nicely with it.

- Turn the table over, then use a hand drill to join each of the four legs.

- Once the legs are joined, flip your table back over.

- The coffee table must be stained as the very last step.

- Apply the colour to the table's four sides, using a thick, dark brown as a base.

- Apply the stain uniformly to the sides using one foam paintbrush, followed by using a towel to wipe up any extra stain.

- And you need to end up with a quite dark brown colour.

- That's it. The project is complete.

3.11 Ocean Resin Art

Supplies

- Painting canvas panels (2 small)
- Hair dryer
- Acrylics paint (deep blue, Bahama blue, ocean blue, and desert sand)
- Disposable work surface, gloves
- Paintbrush
- Disposable brush
- Pour-on resin (envirotex lite)
- Wooden stir sticks,
- White opaque colour pigment
- Small kitchen torch
- Alcohol and dropper
- Small plus large cups

Instructions

- Using a mix of different colours of acrylic paint, quickly brush the paint on in diagonal lines. For the colours to merge with one another, it is crucial to do so before your paint dries.

- The "deepest" portion of the water should be painted beginning at the upper corner of a canvas with the darkest blue shade. Work in diagonal strokes from side to side.

- Next, as you go nearer to the shoreline, diagonally apply your ocean blue paint, slightly mingling it with dark blue paint.

- Bahama blue paint, mixed in with the deeper colours, should be used after that layer.

- Finally, paint a desert sand colour on the beach. Prior to pouring the resin, let the paint completely dry.

- Make careful to lift the canvases off from your worktable by putting some mixing cups beneath before you begin.

- Use a clear measuring cup to combine half an ounce of resin with half an ounce of hardener.

- Transfer into the second measuring cup after stirring for two min. For one further minute, mix using your clean stir stick.

- The resin should be mixed with several drops of sand paint colour.

- Spread the mixture over a portion of the painting that has been painted with sand using the tip of a broad mixing stick.

- Use a tiny kitchen torch and a hair dryer to blast out any air bubbles appearing on the resin's surface after ten to fifteen minutes. Over the following one to two hours, repeat as required. The "water" portion of the artwork should be your target when using a torch or hair dryer.

- Inside a dry measuring cup, combine resin plus hardener in equal parts. For this project, you will require a total of around 4 oz. Transfer into the second measuring cup after stirring for two min. For one further minute, mix using a stir stick.

- Reserve roughly 1 ounce of the resin mixture for the "waves" inside the smaller measuring cup.

- Starting from the cured end of the "sand," pour your clear resin upon the remaining canvas, working your way up to the top.

- Make sure the clear resin completely covers the canvases, going over the sides as well. Continue to the following step.

- The resin should be mixed with several drops of opaque, white-coloured pigment and alcohol.

- Apply unequal diagonal stripes of the white resin mix over the canvas's changing colour areas with the stir stick's tip.

- Use a kitchen torch or hair dryer to blow your white resin mixture as soon as it has been poured, which will cause those white "rushing waves" to diffuse and blend.

- The heat and airflow will produce a wave-like effect that is realistic. As previously said, make sure the dryer is aimed at the peak of the canvas.

- Use a torch/hair dryer to blast off all air bubbles that appear on the resin's surface after 10 to 15 minutes. Over the following one to two hours, repeat as required.

- To prevent dust from gathering, position the cutting boards upon a surface that is level and cover them. Allow healing overnight (twenty-four hours for the soft cure, seventy-two hours for the full cure).

3.12 Marbled Gold Leaf Resin Calligraphy Oblique Holders

Supplies

- Epoxy Modeling Clay (Easy Sculpt)
- Gold Leaf & Adhesive
- Precision Saw

- White Spray paint
- Brass Nib Holders
- Easy Marble Paint

Instructions

- You require an equal number of each pot. The hardener in one portion and the resin in another.
- When it is smooth or not marbling, combine it.
- Although it is quite sticky, it is designed to rest for a time to lessen stickiness and make shaping easier.
- Divide them into bits and let them approximately 20 minutes to sit.
- The desired forms were then created by rolling them. Be inventive and make the gripping portion between 3/4 to an inch in diameter. If the clay becomes too sticky, use cornflour.
- Place parchment paper down for them to rest. They could flatten while they sit if they're still moldable. Rotate them often for one to two hours. After that, let them cure overnight.
- You'll now need a brass flange.

- Cut a slit into the pen holder's end using the precision saw. The middle of the end should be sliced about halfway through.
- The flanges should be inserted and secured with CA thin and otherwise superglue.
- It dries in a matter of seconds.
- Next, apply some painter's tape to the flanges.
- Spray-paint them with a couple of light coats.
- If you desire a distressed appearance, sand down.
- The marbling comes next.
- Paint should be added last, followed by a pin swirl and pen holder. Lean against something to dry.
- If the flanges need to be cleaned, use an acetone-soaked cotton swab.
- Now apply a small amount of gold leaf adhesive where you want it to be coated in gold to the pen holders. Give the adhesive a minute to cure.
- Then apply gold leaf on top. Apply some gold leaf and push with your fingertips.
- The gold leaf which did not stick to the glue should then be removed using a stiff paintbrush.

- After giving them a couple of light coats of lacquer, let them dry overnight.

- You are now prepared to start writing by adding some nibs.

3.13 Casting Clear Resin Paperweights
Supplies

- Casting Resin (Clear Polyester)
- Items to embed (like dandelion, fossils, succulent, and wasp paper)
- Casting Molds

Instructions

- Read the directions on the resin.
- Make certain that you are prepared with all you require.
- Re-read the directions.
- After that, combine the resin as directed on the packaging.
- Pour approximately 1/4 inch into each mould, then allow it to dry till it resembles gel.
- After that, carefully place the object face down into the gelled resin.

- As you'll observe, fresh plants, including succulents and dandelions, will turn brown after hardening.

- Give the resin a few more hours to settle. Then, after thoroughly mixing some more resin, pour it into the mould. Allow it to cure for about a week.

- After that, remove it to enjoy the paperweights! You'll see that the succulent's green tint has faded. It's still incredibly nice, however!

- You will now be searching through your home for fresh items to add to the resin.

- Apply the same method next to a fully bloomed dandelion. Simply place it delicately there in gelled resin...let it settle for a bit.

- The remaining dandelion will then be enclosed by more epoxy added to the mould.

- The resin should be poured in from the side and then allowed to fill in the gaps surrounding the wisps to ensure that the dandelion is held correctly.

- Add roughly half an inch of resin to the mould. Place a sheet of wasp paper on top and use a stick to gently press it in half.

- After drying, remove it.

- These fascinating fossils are the last ones. They are named Crinoids, and although they resemble tiny screws and other machine parts, they are actually a kind of primitive animal, like a sea star. After the resin has dried to a gel-like consistency, just drop these in.

- Pack them full. This is a fantastic way to experience these small, delicate fossils since they are so fragile that breaking them would be quite simple.

- After a few hours, add more resin to cover them thoroughly.

- Allow them to be fully set. They are likely to be hard if they do not smell like resin. Work in a well-ventilated location like the garage.

- Now you may enjoy your paperweights! Send them as gifts and put items that you want to keep within them. Get creative and encapsulate chocolates, your first home key, or even baby teeth.

3.14 Maui's Fishhook Necklace

Supplies

- Epoxy Clay
- Hobby Knife
- Leather cord

Instructions

- There are two parts to epoxy clay. Before starting, carefully read the directions; furthermore, put on gloves because this substance is sticky.

- Take the same amount of clay from each container.

- After that, combine them well, so there is no marbling. The clay is sticky at first, but as it cures, it becomes less sticky.

- It should rest on a parchment-lined surface for twenty to thirty minutes after being formed into a smooth shape.

- After some time in the sitting position, handling and shaping are simple. Allow it to sit a bit longer if it's still too sticky. Read the instructions and keep a tight eye on it because temperature plus climate will affect how it behaves. Next, mould the clay into the shape of a curved hook.

- Cut a little notch with the hobby knife and place it at the hook's point. The epoxy clay dries like ceramic and is smooth.

- Allow it to be completely set, ideally overnight. It has a stunning glossy finish and resembles a real bone hook.

- Create the necklace using the leather cording at this point.

- Tie a square knot after winding the cord centre about four times around your hook's top. Make sure the remaining ends are tied to fit easily around one's head.

- It is now ready to be worn. If you want, you could use a brown Sharpie pen to add tribal emblems and ornaments to it!

3.15 Resin Gold Glitter Brunch Tray
Supplies

- A serving tray.
- Heat gun
- Mod podge
- Gold glitter
- Mixing cups
- Gloves
- High gloss resin (ETI envirotex Lite)

Instructions

- In a single-use plastic cup, combine one portion mod podge and one portion glitter. Stirring is necessary to properly incorporate the glitter. Pour them into the tray next, then tilt and tip your tray to cover the base completely. Wait a minimum of four hours for it to dry. Simply put it away for the night.

- It looks beautiful the next day! It is sparkling and golden, and since the glitter won't flake off everywhere, it's a success. But let's eliminate the grittier glitter texture to make this a win-win situation.

- Only Eight oz of the high gloss finish is utilized. When handling resin, always wear gloves and adhere to the instructions on the packaging.

- It uses a two-part mixing cycle with a 1-to-1 ratio.

- Pour immediately onto the tray following the mixing. The tray should be tilted and tipped so that the base is coated in high gloss resin. Dust can be kept off by covering it with a board. Remove the board after 20 minutes and use your heat gun to eliminate any bubbles which have developed during the curing procedure. After that, swap out the board and give it 24 hours to settle.

- The tray is now as bright as can be and as smooth as glass!

- You may get started by mixing in some hot chocolate and a massive amount of marshmallows.

3.16 Leaf Clover Shamrock Keychain of Resin
Supplies

- Four Leaf Clovers
- Jump rings.

- Easy Cast Resin
- Ball Chain Keychains
- Resin Molds
- Drill/Bit
- Stirring Sticks,
- Disposable Gloves/Worksurface
- Mixing cups

Instructions

- As directed on the packaging, mix the resin. It is critical to correctly measure and mix for the appropriate period of time for the resin once to cure properly. Once combined, pour a little amount of resin into the pendant moulds' bases.
- A single four-leaf clover should be inserted into each pendant once the resin has had 20 minutes to harden.
- After giving them another twenty minutes to cure, add more resin to a mixing bowl and completely fill each mould.
- Give the resin a few days to set and cure.

- Afterwards, remove them from the moulds.
- Create a little hole at the top of every pendant using a drill and bit.
- Jewellery pliers can be used to thread a jump ring through the opening.
- They may then be turned into earrings, strung on the necklace, or attached to the ball chain to make a keychain.
- Put it on your coat.

3.17 Sparrow Wall Art Custom Silicone Mold
Supplies

- Fast Cast
- Mold Silicone Putty

Instructions

- You'll require a different quantity depending on the scope of your project.
- We use a half pound for the smaller bird. The bird is 4 x 3.5 inches in size.
- You want a putty mass that is sufficiently huge to provide a nice border and compensate for the thickness.

- It is packaged as a mixture of one part purple & one part white.
- Once combined, you only have a few minutes to work with putty until it hardens.
- Combine everything and incorporate it completely.
- Then gently flatten to the object's required size.
- Place the item face down over the clay.
- Incorporate gradually.
- Do not fully press it against the table.
- To create a nice mould, you need some cushion beneath.
- Allow it to be totally set. It only requires around thirty minutes.
- After that, you may simply push the object out of the mould.
- Right now, you could absolutely make a nice heirloom chocolate.
- The huge bird, which measures 5.5 x 5 inches, was made with a 1 lb. package of silicone putty.
- Let's cast it now.
- It dries out white. In ten minutes, it sets. It is quick and so much fun!

- It is blended with equal parts of casting resin and hardener.
- Read the instructions completely.
- It requires a two-part mixing step, which must be completed rapidly because the product sets up so quickly.
- Therefore, make sure everything is ready before beginning.
- Fill the silicone moulds carefully.
- It practically hardens in front of your eyes!
- You may insert a wire for hanging or a piece of the paper clip after it becomes firm enough to keep its shape.
- Pull these from the moulds after letting them completely set.
- Correct some of the edges with some small scissors.
- Complete a second rapid cast set and add a droplet of green as well as three drops of a blue opaque colour dye.
- Pouring, mixing, and stirring all take place in the same manner.
- When you pop them out, they rival the original and are ready to be hung.
- They may also be painted in whatever colour you like.

3.18 Bottle Cap Keychains Magnets Pinbacks

Supplies

- Envirotex Jewellery Clay
- Keychain hardware, pinback, or magnets
- Watch parts.
- Bottle Caps

Instructions

- Before starting, ensure you have everything prepared by carefully reading the instructions.
- Each container's component portion must be used once.
- They should be thoroughly combined after being combined.
- Clay should be cut into bits.
- Make sure the bottle tops are filled and not inflated by pressing into them.
- Place tiny watch components or rhinestones within clay using fingers or a pair of tweezers. Then for the clay to finish drying. Being prepared is essential for this activity because the jewellery clay hardens in around twenty minutes. After that, attach magnets or pinbacks to the back using E6000 adhesive.
- Allow the adhesive to fully cure.

- They are then prepared to wear, stand out, or flaunt!

3.19 Gold Leaf & Emerald Cabinet Knobs
Supplies

- Gold leaf
- Baking sheet
- Knob hardware
- Surface for working.
- E6000 glue
- Wood board

Instructions

- Read the directions on your casting resin properly.
- The instructions on how much hardener to add are a little ambiguous.
- Mix an entire cup of resin all at once.
- However, you only need enough to first fill ½ of your moulds.
- Although mould release spray is an option, ones come out absolutely fine without it.
- Half-fill the moulds.

- Place other objects on top of the mould to straighten it up while it was curing because it had a slight bend in it.
- Give it roughly an hour to sit.
- Even though it won't be fully set, it will resemble gel and be prepared for leafing.
- Just roll and rip up the leafing, using less than a sheet.
- It would be simpler if you had gold leaf flakes.
- Just fill the moulds with leaf flakes & rolls.
- Simply let it aside for another hour.
- Combine a bit more resin now (inside a new cup using a fresh stirring stick)
- Add several drops of the green resin colour and create just enough for the moulds.
- Since it is translucent rather than opaque, the gold leaf would still be seen.
- After that, carefully pour over the top of your gold leaf, filling the mould to the top.
- After then, let it sit in peace for several days.
- To make sure it has cured, let it sit for a week.
- Remove them from the mould and let them a few more days to settle.

- Since they still smelled somewhat like resin.
- The green resin now blended with the resin and turned them all emerald.
- They wouldn't have appeared as wonderful if there had been a sharp, clear, colourful line.
- Just sand the undersides smoothly if they are a little uneven and contain a few rough edges.
- They would seem flawless after being sanded and cleaned off.
- We then use E6000, and our cabinet pulls hardware.
- Put a little amount of glue upon the hardware and afterwards carefully place it on the knobs' backs.
- The surfaces appear rounded; lay them over bubble wrap to keep them straight.
- Give them a minimum of four hours to dry.
- They are prepared for use once the machine screw is added.

3.20 Resin Agate Slices
Supplies

- Polyester Casting Resin
- Disposable Gloves
- Gold Leaf Paint
- Translucent Dyes
- Nail File
- Silicone Caulking
- Paintbrush
- Parchment Paper

Instructions

- Start by wrapping parchment paper over a sturdy surface.
- Next, create rings by nesting one round circle within the next using silicone caulk. Allow them to totally dry or cure. Let it sit for an entire night; it would be rubbery.
- The resin is then required. For each colour of resin you wish to create, use a tiny mixing cup with a stirring stick in addition to a big mixing cup & stirring stick.
- To mix and handle the resin, read, and stick by the directions on the packaging.
- 4.5 ounces of resin are combined.

- Divide them into 7 distinct little cups, then combine them with a few drops of translucent dyes.

- After that, fill the rings upon the parchment that is open with resin. Give them about an hour to set.

- The silicone rings should then be carefully removed from the resin's centre. Keep the outer ring in place.

- Allow the resin to cure overnight.

- Prepare extra clear casting resin the next day. Pour over the coloured rings, fill the spaces in between the rings, and then allow to cure one more overnight.

- The next day, remove the silicone outer ring and peel the paper with the attached agate slices.

- Each slice's edges should be sanded and made smooth with a nail file.

- The edges of slices should then be painted gold using some liquid Leaf.

- They may be used as décor, accent pieces, coasters, and more when totally dried.

3.21 Tree Branch Jewellery Organizer
Supplies

- Tree Branch
- E6000 glue

- Log Slice

- Gold Spray Paint

- Epoxy Resin

- Gloves

- Paintbrush

- Stirring sticks

- Disposable work surface

- Mixing cups

Instructions

- Find the ideal tree branch first.

- Find a method to suspend the branch over the disposable napkin upside down. Fasten the branch clothes-pinned to light without a bulb.

- In accordance with the instructions on the packaging, combine 2 ounces of resin. After that, coat the branch with resin using the paintbrush. The paintbrush would also be ruined and drip into the tablecloth.

- After it has been dripping for several minutes, use a stirring stick to scrape the resin from the surface and reattach it to the branch. More resin is better since it will help support and strengthen the branch.

- After that, give it a minimum of 24 hours to properly dry and cure.

- Spray-paint the branch completely gold or copper.

- Drill a hole into the base of the log slice that is the exact size of the branch's base.

- Place the stick directly into the hole after adding some E6000 adhesive. It must dry for around 4 hours before being prepared for use.

- Stylishly keeps a record of all that lost jewellery.

- It's adorable and functional as house décor.

3.22 Lace Pendants
Supplies

- EnviroTex Jewelry Resin
- Pendant Bezel plus chain
- UltraSeal/ ModPodge

Instructions

- Step one is to prepare a lace piece that fits snugly inside the bezel.

- Next, generously coat the bezel with sealant.

- Put the lace over the top, then cover it with sealant.

- In a two-phase process, combine the resin as directed on the packaging. As the hanging portion extends towards the back, raise the bezel toward a level surface.

- After that, slowly pour a little amount of resin into the bezel.

- Up till the resin bubbles from over the edge at the top and holds on along with surface tension. After letting it stand for around fifteen minutes, gently blow all the created bubbles with a straw. After that, let it 24 hours to cure.

- As a necklace, the lace is charming and delicate.

- If you want a bolder contrast, insert and seal a round of black cardboard before the lace in the begel.

3.23 Mermaid Tail Resin Keychains
Supplies

- Easy cast resin
- Stirring sticks
- Mermaid-tailed silicone molds
- Mixing cups
- Glitter
- Keychain hardware

- Gloves
- Drill and bit
- Disposable workspace
- Transparent dyes

Instructions

- Follow the instructions on the EasyCast packaging before mixing. The moulds are placed inside a cardboard box.
- Use 2 droplets of blue dye plus 1 droplet of green dye in an ounce of resin to create the ideal aqua.
- Combine well after mixing.
- Fill the mermaid tail mould with liquid.
- Just the right amount of resin was present in one ounce to thoroughly fill both the larger and smaller tails up towards the fin transition.
- After that, take your fine glitter and cover the moulds with it.
- The glitter will disperse and sink into the resin.
- The next day, let them dry, then set them. The following day, prepare more resin and maintain it clear. The huge mermaid tail's last fin should be filled. Once more, let them sit overnight to cure.

- Remove the mermaid tails from the moulds to reveal their shimmer.

- Drill holes at the top of every single mermaid tail using a tiny drill bit.

- Fill the hole with a bead chain.

- Add a keychain clasp and. Our mermaid tails are prepared to keep sight of keys or appear gorgeous on a rucksack.

- They gleam and dazzle! These mermaids-tailed keychains are ideal for summertime activities and party treats.

3.24 Resin Succulent Garden
Supplies

- Resin Succulents
- Pink Craft Paint
- Large Pink Pot
- Stuffing (Polyfil)
- Small Clay Pot
- Crushed Mirror Glass

Instructions

- We must first prepare a little bit before setting up your little succulent garden. In order to match your large clay pot, start by painting a small clay pot a bright blush pink. Don't forget to paint the inside as well, as some of it might show. Then let it dry.

- We should now fill the pot! Take a completely different route because we don't want to load the entire pot using expensive smashed glass. Now stuff the pot to the full of filling, covering the whole surface area. As you set something on the filling, this would sink down a little (similar to how a pillow dips under your head), therefore, keep adding stuffing till it feels reasonably secure within your pot.

- It is now time to move forward. Place your smaller pink pot within your bigger pink pot right away. Place your pot directly beneath the centre of the pot since you don't need it to be exactly in the centre (your succulents would be in the precise centre).

- Imagine that your pot's surface is divided into thirds. Put your little pot in the space between the bottom and centre third.

- It wasn't enjoyable for me to shift mine down a little.

- After your pot is in place, start adding smashed glass to the top. You should also add some crushed glass to the pot. Next, enclose the sides. Make sure that all of the small whispy are covered with broken glass and that no stuffing is visible so that the crushed glass would weigh down your stuffing a little (which is excellent!).

- The best part is finally here, adding our succulents! Choose a couple of faves from the collection of resin succulents; however, you can use the whole method to build a handful of your own if you have no stockpile. If you've never worked before with resin before, don't let this stop you from trying it out because it's a quick and simple project (ideal for beginners).

- After your succulents are prepared, begin with the bigger pieces. Placed the largest succulent against the flat succulent that was in the little pot (just peeping out from beneath the rim).

- In order to make an arrangement which spills over the sides and covers the top, uses the succulents from this side in a variety of shapes and colours.

3.25 Faceted Gem Magnets
Supplies

- Clear casting resin 3.5 oz
- Wooden stir stick

- 14 drops colourant (may also use resin tint, acrylic, or alcohol ink)
- 2-part epoxy
- Black glitter 8-10 tbsp
- A plastic cup is needed for mixing.
- Silicone mold (gem shaped)
- Drop cloth for protecting the work surface.
- Strong and thin magnets
- Apron
- Safety glasses
- Cutting board/ solid surface (for setting silicone mold for stability)
- Gloves

Instructions

- Creating resin magnets turned out to be quite simple.! If possible, complete this project outdoors or in a garage with good ventilation (just go through the instructions to ensure the temperature becomes correct). It may be messy to make resin magnets. I you spill any, then apparently, cleanup is really challenging. Put on some old clothing, safety glasses, and gloves to safeguard your worktable.

- It will be simpler to transport your item to a different location to let it set if you first lay the silicone mould on a solid, flat surface (like one cutting board). Use one plastic mixing cup (take anything from the trash or recycling) and the wooden stir stick to combine the casting resin plus catalyst (sold together yet separated). The directions will be on the can, so strictly abide by them! After that, gently pour the mixture into a silicone mould after stirring in glitter as well as a small amount of colourant (we chose black). Let it sit there for several minutes before moving it into the fish room to enable it to be properly set there without being disturbed. After several days, when it fully hardened, mix up 2-part epoxy and then attach a strong, flat magnet towards the back.
- Adorable resin magnets in the form of gems are created.

3.26 Beaded resin Letter
Supplies

- Box cutter
- Drinking straw
- Paper mache letter
- Assorted beads
- White acrylic paint
- Rubber gloves

- Paintbrush
- 2 Disposable containers
- Mod podge
- Hot glue gun containing glue.
- Foam brush
- Pourable resin (we use approximately 24 ounces of mixed resin, i.e. twelve ounces of epoxy and twelve ounces of hardener)
- Scissors
- Cardboard box big enough to cover the letter.
- Wooden paint stirrers 2
- wooden craft sticks (large)
- A garbage bag/ plastic drop cloth

Instructions

- Remove the chipboard letter's front panel and any inside pieces using the box cutter to create one hollow chipboard letter.
- Apply two or three coats of white paint to the letter. Allow the required time for the paint to dry in between coats.

- Use a foam brush to apply a considerate coating of mod podge to each letter. Permit the mod podge to dry fully.

- Set up your work area for pouring resin. Put on your gloves and put a clean garbage bag and otherwise plastic drop cloth onto a level surface.

- The first twelve oz. Of resin should be prepared pursuant to packaging instructions. In general, this entails combining an equal proportion of epoxy resin plus epoxy hardener inside a disposable container using the wooden paint stirrer and perhaps a sizable wooden craft stick, whereupon stirring slowly (to help prevent bubbles) for almost five minutes.

- Add resin to every letter halfway. Cover the letters using a cardboard box if you want to prevent dust or other debris from falling into the resin. Cure the resin as instructed on the box.

- Get rid of your used mixing tools. Don't use it again for the upcoming batch of resin.

- When the resin has finally cured, directly glue your beads onto the resin using your hot glue gun.

- Prepare the remainder 12 ounces of resin per the previous instructions, then slowly pour it over the beads until the letter is covered. Avoid overfilling.

- If bubbles are present, carefully blow through a straw while hovering over the bubbles.

- A box should be used to cover the letter, and before displaying, allow the resin to completely cure.

3.27 Colorful layered Pencil Holder

Supplies

- Clear Casting Epoxy
- Drill
- Stir Sticks
- Latex Gloves
- Disposable Measuring Cups
- Square Mold
- Protective Eyewear
- Micro-butane torch (this is optional)
- Mold Release & Conditioner
- Casting Resin Craft Spray Finish
- Paints (of various colours)
- Drill bit, similar size or bit larger than a pen or pencil

Instructions

- Apply a small spray of Conditioning Spray and Mold Release into your mould, then let it dry. Add another layer. Once the resin has dried and hardened, your mould is now ready for usage.

- As this project calls for many resin layers, you will be combining equal parts of Casting Epoxy Parts A & B for every layer. Let's construct this pencil holder while using latex gloves and safety glasses!

- You must add 1/4 ounce of Part A to a designated measuring cup. After that, add the identical quantity of Part B (also 1/4 ounce) to the same cup.

- It takes a moment or two to combine them completely.

- After carefully mixing once again, pour the liquid into the second clean cup. The two-cup approach is used, which guarantees that all of the resin is well blended.

- Your paint colour should then be added. Each paint colour received roughly five droplets, but the quantity you use would depend upon the viscosity of the paints. Use several drops and mix; next, add more if required to achieve the desired colour. You wish to use as small an amount as possible. The resin won't cure if there is too much paint added.

- Prepare to pour after completely incorporating the colour.

- Slowly pour the resin into the middle of your mould. Your resin will cover the bottom evenly.

- Let the resin settle for several minutes before using the micro-butane torch so as to blow out the air bubbles.

- Let this layer at a minimum of 24 hours to cure. Cover it with a heavy object to prevent dust from landing while it's still curing.

- Repeat the same steps for the 2nd through the 6th layers, only changing the colours you add every time. Wait a minimum of 24 hours among layers so that they may cure properly. The blending and pouring will proceed quite rapidly. Even though it takes several days to complete, this project isn't particularly time-consuming.

- After pouring each layer, don't forget to burst the bubbles and let them cure.

- Make a bit extra resin for the last layer so that it is thicker. Totally fill the mould, but you might not wish to do that as it makes it a little trickier to get the product out of the form when it cures. It's purely a matter of preference.

- Once more, blow out every bubble, then give it a minimum of 24 hours to cure. This time left it for forty-eight hours to make sure the whole piece was fully cured. If the piece is difficult to remove from the mould after 24 hours, it could only require a little extra curing time. In the centre portion of your last layer, capture a good shot of the bubbles popping.

- Take the mould off of the square pencil holder. Large parts in a complete mould like this might make this a bit challenging but be patient as you pull the edges away out from the resin. Once your air seal has been broken, it will rather simply release. Insert a small knife blade into one side to break that seal, and it immediately popped out.

- You now own a resin block containing layers of colour. It's time to make it a real pencil holder.

- Take your drill and the appropriate size drill bit, and let's get started.

- Wherever the holes should be, start softly drilling into the resin. Decide to make four holes, 2 of each size.

- You'll observe that as you drill, the resin shavings start to take on the colours of resin layers.

- Drill up till the colour of the next-to-last layer.

- Next, drill the remaining holes. Instead of sawdust, brush all the resin particles now and apply one thin layer of resin spray.

- That's all there is to it! A bright and sparkling pencil holder!

3.28 Resin Bookmarks

Supplies

- Bookmark silicone molds
- Flowers
- Epoxy resin
- Optional: Tassles
- Optional: Any other stuff you may wish to add (gilded foil flakes, tint, buttons, glitter, sequins, etc.)

Instructions

- Be sure to strictly adhere to the instructions while dealing with resin so that you are using the proper ratios and know how long you will work with it.

- The resin used will have a 1:1 ratio, so it can only be worked with for around 40 minutes before becoming rigid. You only need to be quick since it takes 18 to 24 hours to be cured. It shouldn't be difficult, as we're dealing with tiny bookmarks.

- There is an A and B portion, and most resin functions the same way in both. Pour the components into a cup after measuring.

- Using a popsicle stick, thoroughly combine the two components. Reusable materials are ideal for this project because eating or drinking from items coated in resin looks on brand but is not great for daily health.

- Here, you would add any mix-ins, such as gilded gold flakes, colour, glitter, or other materials. The time has not yet come to add your flowers.

- Resin should be poured into the moulds.

- Cut your flowers into small, tiny pieces using scissors. They are the ideal size if you have little flowers, such as baby breath or the like. Make sure any bigger flowers or foliage are tiny enough to submerge entirely in your resin if you intend to utilize them.

- Use old tweezers pair to push it down through into the resin.

- Put them aside for drying. Put them onto paper plates to move them quickly.

- Afternoon preparation allowed them to sit for a full twenty-four hours.

- After you remove the bookmarks from your mould, you will have stunning resin art, which you can keep as a memento of your memorable occasion, containing your preserved flowers.

3.29 Wood Bookend

Supplies

- Chunk of wood

- Resin Spray (High Gloss)

- EasyCast Resin

- Mold which fits the wood

- Sandpaper in different grits

- Transparent resin dye

Instructions

- Start by preparing a resin mixture that will fill half of the mould. You must carefully read and adhere to the directions on the packaging. Use gloves, work on a disposable surface, and be safe. Well, so the ratio is 1 part resin to 1 part hardener. Pour into the second mixing cup, then stir for an additional minute after mixing for two minutes. The resin is then poured into the mould. After allowing it to set for thirty min, carefully lay the wood piece over the top of your clear resin. Let it cure all night.

- You may now remove the wood plus resin from the mould.

- The following step combines the same volume of Resin as before with a few droplets of transparent dye. You can use green. Just like before, pour it into the mould and set it for 20 to 30 minutes.

- Next, position the resin plus wood directly atop your green resin. Remove your wood and resin after letting it set for the night.

- Quickly take your resin to sander and create several sharp edges and surfaces. Sand randomly till the resin becomes very crystalline.

- The sanding procedure will start after that. Sand each edge with each grit for approximately five minutes.

- Sand very edge with 150 grit.

- Next, 240 grit.

- Next comes 320 grits.

- After which 400 grit.

- To 600 grits now.

- Following 1000 grit.

- Followed by 1200 grit.

- 1500 grit comes next.

- Afterwards came the 2000 grit, and at the end, 3000 grit, too.

- To get it extremely smooth, you may sand it all day.

- Instead, spritz Gloss finish on it quickly.

- The resin seems crystal clear and beautiful after one treatment.
- This resin bookend's geometric design is gorgeous! Create two of these to have a pair, or simply stack your books flat and place one on top to serve as a paperweight.

3.30 Confetti Resin Tray
Supplies

- High Gloss Finish
- Scissors/ Paper Slicer
- Colourful cardstock
- Drill
- Wooden frame
- Mixing Cups
- Drawer Pulls
- Stir Sticks

Instructions

- Start by measuring and marking the handles on the wooden frame. First, drill holes and attach them.
- A paper cutter or scissors may be used to create your confetti. This may also be done using a rotary cutter.

- Confetti should be evenly distributed on the tray's bottom. If necessary, add more to ensure the bottom is completely covered and is thickly stacked.

- Get the resin ready. Don't begin mixing unless you are prepared to complete the entire procedure from beginning to end because it is a multi-stage process!

- Combine the resin and the hardener in equal amounts.

- Gently whisk for 2 minutes (make sure to scrape the sides and bottoms), then pour out from the initial cup into the other and mix for another minute using a fresh stir stick.

- Time to start pouring now! Pour onto the dish and thoroughly around the confetti! Ensure all your paper is thoroughly coated and add additional resin if necessary to get the desired thickness.

- The tray is prepared for use after the resin has had time to cure.

Conclusion

Resin crafts have become increasingly popular throughout the last century, becoming a household activity in many countries worldwide.

Handmade gifts—whether they are for you or someone else, show attention and care in today's quick-fix, disposable consumer world and have a value which no mass-produced product can. And then, there is the art crafting process. When you stop to think about it, many of the advantages are obvious: it offers you an opportunity to use your hands, it's indeed lovely to your sensation, and when you complete a project, that's something to be proud of. Everyone who already engages in resin art or any other forms of creativity will be aware of this, given their participation in the crafting and artistic communities.

BONUS TIME

Discover the best projects in amazing tutorial videos here!

Exclusive eBook - The 12 Steps to Begin you must absolutely know

Made in United States
North Haven, CT
22 May 2023